Where's the Bear

A Look-and-Find Book

The J. Paul Getty Museum · Los Angeles

About This Book

All the pictures here come from *The Entry of the Animals into Noah'sArk,* a painting in the Getty Museum. It was made by the artist Jan Brueghel. (You pronounce his name "Yahn **Broy**-gul"; the letters in **boldface** tell you which part of the word to stress.)

Jan Brueghel has included more than fifty different animals; we've picked out twenty-three. Now see if you can find them in the painting. (It's in the back of the book.)

We've provided the name of each animal in English. Just for fun, we added the animal names in other languages too.

Do you know how to say *bat* in Italian or *elephant* in Japanese? You'll soon find out!

But first . . .

Cerf
Sair
French

Hirsch
Heersh
German

Where's the Deer?

Cervo
Chehr - vo
Italian

シカ
Shi - **ka**
Japanese

Ciervo
See - **air** - vo
Spanish

Here.

Cochon

Ko - **show**

French

Schwein

Shvine

German

Maiale

Mah - **yah** - leh

Italian

ブタ

Bu - **ta**

Japanese

Cerdo

Ser - doh

Spanish

Pig

Swan

Cygne

See - nyuh

French

Schwan

Shvahn

German

Cigno

Chee - nyoh

Italian

ハクチョウ

Ha - ku - **cho**

Japanese

Cisne

Sees - neh

Spanish

Eléphant

Ay - lay - **faw**

French

Elefant

Eh - leh - **fahnt**

German

Elepha

Elefante

Eh - leh - **fahn** - teh

Italian

ゾウ

Zoh

Japanese

Eléfante

Eh - leh - **fahn** - teh

Spanish

Hibou

Ee - **boo**

French

Eule

Oi - leh

German

Civetta

Chee - **vet** - tah

Italian

フクロウ

Fu - **ku** - ru

Japanese

Lechuza

Leh - **choo** - sah

Spanish

Owl

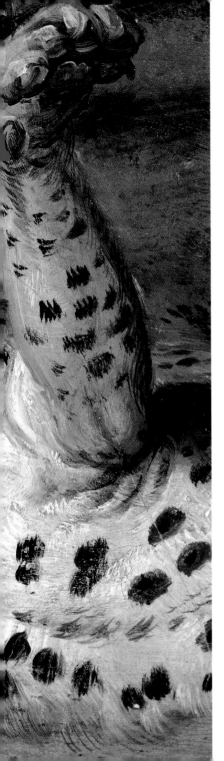

Léopard

Leh - oh - **par**

French

Leopard

Leh - oh - **pahrd**

German

Leopardo

Leh - oh - **par** - doh

Italian

ヒョウ

Hyoh

Japanese

Leopardo

Leh - oh - **par** - doh

Spanish

Leopard

Autruche

O - **trewsh**

French

Strauß

Shtrouse

German

Ostrich

Struzzo

Stroo - tso

Italian

ダチョウ

Da - **cho**

Japanese

Avestruz

Ah - ve**s** - **troos**

Spanish

Bat

Chauve-souris

Showv - soo - **ree**

French

Pipistrello

Pee - pee - **strehl** - lo

Italian

コウモリ

Ko - mo - ri

Japanese

Fledermaus

Camel

Chameau

Shah - mo

French

Kamel

Kah - mail

German

Cammello

Kahm - mel - lo

Italian

ラクダ

Ra - ku - dah

Japanese

Camello

Kah - meh - yo

Spanish

Tortue

Tor - **tew**

French

Schildkröte

Shild - krur - teh

German

Tartaruga

Tar - ta - **roo** - ga

Italian

カメ

Ka - meh

Japanese

Tortuga

Tor - **too** - gah

Spanish

Tortoise

Goat

Chèvre

Shev - ruh

French

Ziege

Tsee - geh

German

Capra

Kah - prah

Italian

ヤギ

Ya - gi

Japanese

Cabra

Kah - brah

Spanish

Chat

Shah

French

Katze

Kah - tseh

German

Gatto

Gaht - toh

Italian

Cat

ネコ

Ne - ko

Japanese

Gato

Gah - toh

Spanish

Porcupine

Porc-épic
Por - ke - **peek**

French

Stachelschwein
Shtakh - el - shvine

German

Porcospino
Por - ko - **spee** - no

Italian

ヤマアラシ
Ya - ma - **ah** - ra - shi

Japanese

Puerco espín
Pwair - ko   es - **peen**

Spanish

Lion

Lion
Lee - **yaw**
French

Löwe
Lur - veh
German

Leone
Leh - **oh** - neh
Italian

ライオン
Ra - **ee** - on
Japanese

León
Leh - **ohn**
Spanish

Dindon

Dan - **daw**

French

Tacchino

Tah - **kee** - no

Italian

Truthahn

Troot - hahn

German

シチメンチョウ

Shi - chi - **men** - cho

Japanese

Pavo

Pah - vo

Spanish

Turkey

Bull

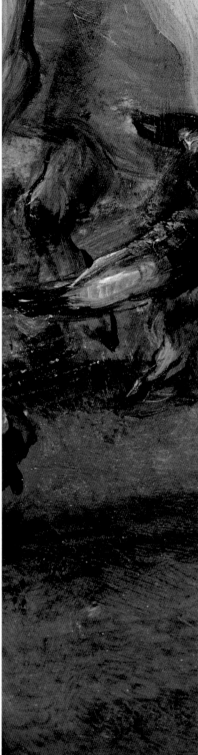

Taureau
Toh - **roh**

French

Stier
Shteer

German

Toro
Toh - roh

Italian

ウシ
U - **shi**

Japanese

Toro
Toh - roh

Spanish

Parrot

Perroquet

Pair - o - **kay**

French

Papagei

Pah - pah - **guy**

German

Pappagallo

Pahp - pah - **gahl** - lo

Italian

オウム

O - **mu**

Japanese

Papagayo

Pah - pah - **guy** - yo

Spanish

Chien

She - yeh

French

Hund

Hoont

German

Cane

Kah - neh

Italian

イヌ

E - nu

Japanese

Dog

Perro

Pehr - ro

Spanish

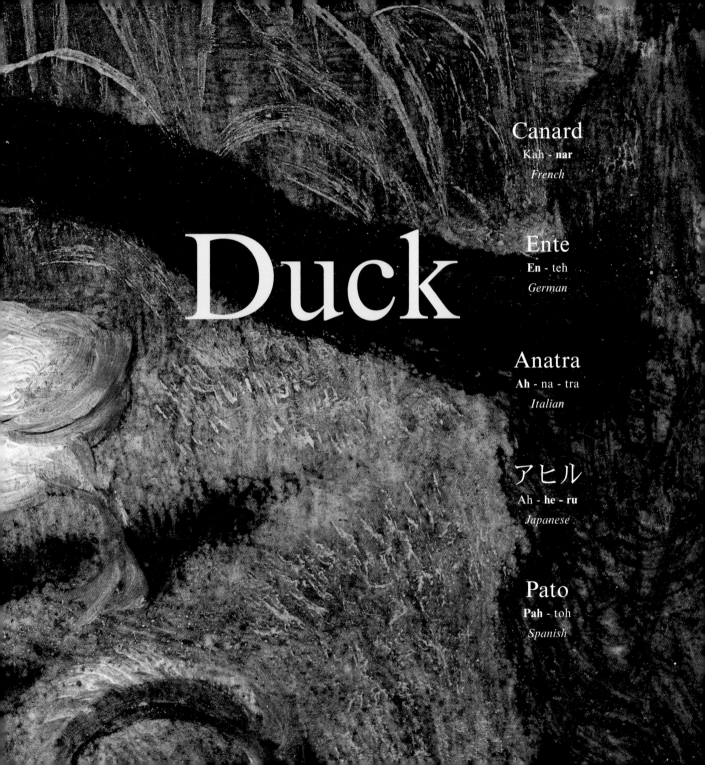

Duck

Canard
Kah - **nar**
French

Ente
En - teh
German

Anatra
Ah - na - tra
Italian

アヒル
Ah - **he** - **ru**
Japanese

Pato
Pah - toh
Spanish

Cheval

Sheh - **vahl**

French

Horse

Pferd

Pfehrd

German

Cavallo

Kah - **vahl** - lo

Italian

ウマ

U - **ma**

Japanese

Caballo

Kah - **buy** - yo

Spanish

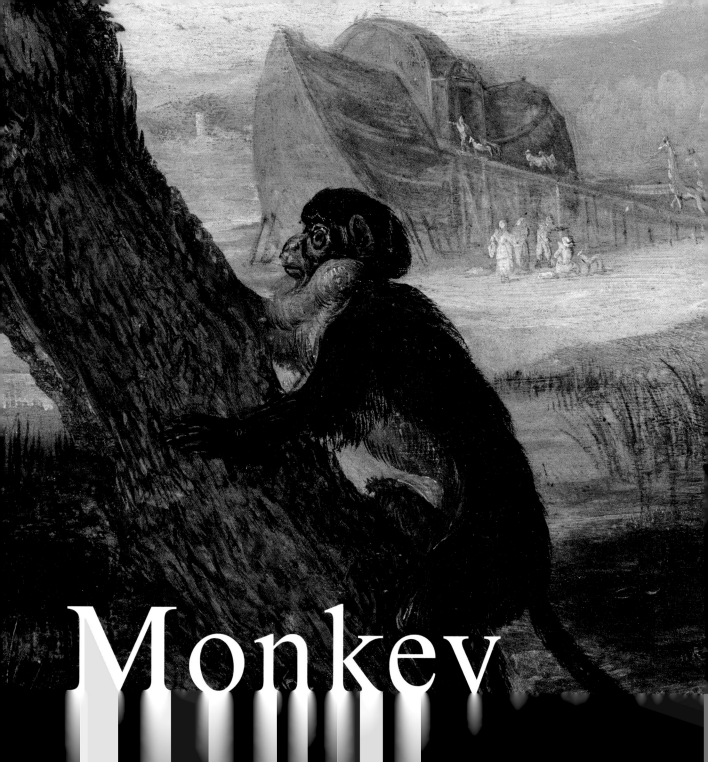

Monkey

Singe

Senj

French

Affe

Ah - feh

German

Scimmia

Sheem - mya

Italian

サル

Sa - ru

Japanese

Mono

Mo - no

Spanish

Lapin

La - **pan**

French

Hase

Ha - zeh

German

Coniglio

Ko - **nee** - lyo

Italian

ウサギ

U - **sa** - **gi**

Japanese

Conejo

Ko - **neh** - ho

Spanish

Rabbit

Where's the **Bear**?

Ours
Oors
French

Bär
Behr
German

Orso
Or - so
Italian

クマ
Ku - ma
Japanese

Oso
O - so
Spanish

There.

About Noah and His Ark

Jan Brueghel painted this picture in 1613. It shows a scene from the story of Noah.

According to the Bible, the world had become so wicked that God decided to send a great flood to destroy every living thing. He spared only Noah and his family, telling Noah to build a huge boat, or ark, and to keep in it two of every animal in the world, male and female.

Jan Brueghel the Elder (Flemish, 1568–1625). *The Entry of the Animals into Noah's Ark,* 1613. Oil on panel, 54.6 x 83.8 cm (21 1/2 x 33 in.). Los Angeles, J. Paul Getty Museum 92.PB.82.

© 1997 The J. Paul Getty Museum 1200 Getty Center Drive Suite 1000 Los Angeles, CA 90049-1687
Christopher Hudson, Publisher Mark Greenberg, Managing Editor
Project Staff: John Harris, Writer and Editor Charles Passela, Photographer
Kurt Hauser, Designer Suzanne Watson Petralli, Production Coordinator
Special thanks to Charles P. (bravissimo!), Arianne Faber-Kolb, Agnew Tech-II, Lazar and Associates, Berlitz Translation Services, Bernard A. Meyer, and Mariko Bird
ISBN 0-89236-378-9
Library of Congress Catalog Card Number: 96-39856
Printed by Tien Wah Press, Singapore